04/05

D1154420

-2

ECOSYSTEMS

Life in a
Desert

Stuart A. Kallen

**KIDHAVEN
PRESS**™

THOMSON

™

GALE

San Diego • Detroit • New York • San Francisco • Cleveland
New Haven, Conn. • Waterville, Maine • London • Munich

Picture Credits

Cover: © Royalty-Free/CORBIS
© Anthony Bannister; Gallo Images/CORBIS, 30, 37 (inset)
© John Borthwick/Lonely Planet Images, 37
© Dean Conger/CORBIS, 29, 33
COREL Corporation, 10 (upper left, bottom), 18 (both), 23, 25 (both), 26 (insets), 34, 41 (inset)
© Richard Cummins/CORBIS, 17
© Ric Ergenbright/CORBIS, 20
© Darrell Gulin/CORBIS, 15
Chris Jouan, 9, 10, 26
© David Muench/CORBIS, 13
© Pierre Perrin/CORBIS SYGMA, 38
PhotoDisc, 5, 6-7, 31, 41
© Adriane Van Zandbergen/Lonely Planet Images, 40

© 2004 by KidHaven Press. KidHaven Press is an imprint of The Gale Group, Inc., a division of Thomson Learning, Inc.

KidHaven™ and Thomson Learning™ are trademarks used herein under license.

For more information, contact
KidHaven Press
27500 Drake Rd.
Farmington Hills, MI 48331-3535
Or you can visit our Internet site at http://www.gale.com

LIBRARY OF CONGRESS CATALOGING-IN-PUBLICATION DATA

Kallen, Stuart A., 1955–
     Life in a desert / by Stuart A. Kallen.
   p. cm. — (Ecosystems)
Summary: Explores the desert ecosystem, discussing where deserts are found, how a desert develops, and how plants, animals, and people survive in this harsh environment.
Includes bibliographical references and index.
  ISBN 0-7377-1530-8 (hardback : alk. paper)
  1. Deserts—Juvenile literature. 2. Desert ecology—Juvenile literature. [1. Deserts.
2. Desert ecology. 3. Ecology.] I. Title. II. Series.
  QH88.K25 2004
  577.54—dc22
                                                     2003012158

Printed in the United States of America

Contents

Chapter 1

Deserts of the World

The word *desert* brings to mind images of scorching-hot sand and bones bleaching in the sun. Although it is true that some deserts are filled with endless, drifting sands, others are marked by towering mountains, beautiful rocks and minerals, and stark landscapes. Deserts may be some of the most forbidding places on Earth, but they are found on every **continent**. Twenty percent, or one-fifth, of the earth's surface is desert.

Deserts are defined by scientists as places where less than ten inches of rain falls every year. Some deserts get far less, however. For example, the parched Atacama Desert in northern Chile and Peru receives less than one inch of rain a year.

Most deserts have very high daytime temperatures. The hottest temperature ever registered on Earth is 136 degrees Fahrenheit. This temperature was recorded in 1922 in the Sahara Desert in Libya. Although that was a one-day record, the average daily temperature in the region in the summer is 110 degrees. Heat blasts of 120 to 130 degrees are not uncommon. A person caught in this baking **environment** without water or shelter can die in only six hours.

Deserts are found on every continent and they take up 20 percent of the earth's surface.

Not all deserts are hot, however. Some, such as the Gobi in China and the Great Basin in the western United States are "cold deserts." In these places, winter temperatures may only be in the forty-degree range during the day and plunge well below freezing at night. Storms can dump several inches of fluffy snow, leaving a fine coating on rocks and cacti.

Ocean Currents Prevent Rain

All deserts, no matter where they are located, have one thing in common. They get little **precipitation** (rain, sleet, and snow) because of various natural barriers and weather conditions.

Deserts are very dry, receiving less than ten inches of rain per year.

Surprisingly, the huge bodies of water that make up the oceans create conditions that produce some of the driest regions in the world. As the earth spins, the oceans make currents that are like rivers of moving water. These currents are very cold because they flow from the North and South Poles toward the center of the earth, called the **equator**. Although warm seawater **evaporates** and forms rain clouds when the sun hits it, the water from the poles is so cold that it does not evaporate. When these currents flow past land, there is no rain to water the deserts.

In South America, the cold Peru Current produces the arid conditions responsible for the Atacama Desert. The Canaries Current works with the Benguela Current to keep the Sahara dry. These currents also

affect the Kalahari Desert in the African country of Botswana. The California Current prevents much rain from falling in southern California.

Hot Winds Create Deserts

In places where there are not cold currents, the earth's rotation creates hot winds along the equator. These winds are called air masses. These air masses starve equatorial deserts of moisture. This hot, dry air helps heat two large belts of deserts above and below the equator.

The northern deserts include the Gobi in China and the Arabian and Iranian Deserts in the Middle East. Southern deserts include the Patagonian Desert in southern Argentina and the Great Victoria and Great Sandy Deserts of Australia.

Mountain Rain Shadows

Some deserts are formed by tall mountains that act as natural barriers to prevent rain clouds from passing over them. For example, towering, snowcapped mountains are often covered with lush forests and raging rivers. Weather conditions in mountains, however, prevent rain clouds from passing over the high peaks. This creates deserts by what is known as the "rain-shadow" effect.

A good example of the rain-shadow effect may be seen in the Sierra Nevada mountains in California and the Cascade Range in Washington, where rain-laden clouds blow in from the Pacific Ocean. As these clouds

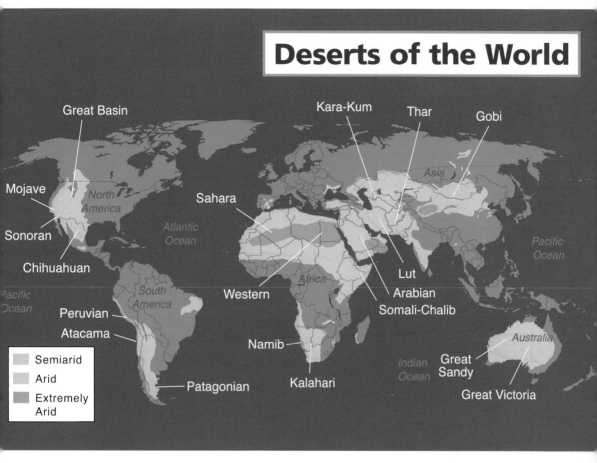

Deserts of the World

Great Basin

Kara-Kum   Thar   Gobi

Mojave

Asia

North
America

Sahara

Sonoran

Atlantic
Ocean

Pacific
Ocean

Chihuahuan

Pacific
Ocean

South
America

Africa

Lut

Western

Arabian

Peruvian

Somali-Chalib

Atacama

Namib

Australia

Semiarid

Great
Sandy

Arid

Indian
Ocean

Extremely
Arid

Patagonian

Kalahari

Great Victoria

move from west to east and try to pass over the mountains, they rise higher in the air, where temperatures are much colder. The cold forces the clouds to dump their moisture. This provides up to one hundred inches of rain per year on some western slopes of the mountains. When the clouds descend on the eastern side of the peaks, however, they no longer have rain for the arid land.

The rain-shadow effect created the Great Basin desert east of the Sierras and the Cascades. The Great Basin is huge, spreading across California, Nevada,

The Rain-Shadow Effect

Windward Side

Moist air over large bodies of water is pushed eastward by massive global air currents. When this air hits the mountains it is forced up the range where it cools, condenses, and falls as rain or snow.

Annual precipitation on the windward side of the Sierra Nevada mountains in California (pictured) averages thirty-five to fifty-five inches per year.

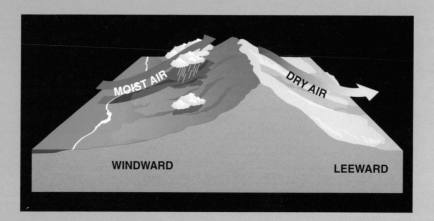

MOIST AIR

DRY AIR

WINDWARD

LEEWARD

Leeward Side

Air that rushes over the top of the mountains and down the other side has lost much of its moisture, creating the arid desert terrain.

Annual precipitation on the leeward side of the Sierra Nevada mountains in California (pictured) is less than ten inches.

Utah, Oregon, and Washington. Cities in the Great Basin get very little precipitation, with Reno, Nevada, receiving seven inches of rain annually and Las Vegas little more than four inches.

Polar Deserts

Some of the driest places on Earth are rarely thought of as deserts. But the Arctic region, around the North Pole, and Antarctica, near the South Pole, are as arid as the Sahara Desert.

The polar deserts are battered by high winds and incredibly cold temperatures that can drop to nearly seventy degrees below zero in the winter and rarely climb above freezing in the summer. These brutal weather conditions prevent much precipitation from falling. And although the poles are covered with ice and snow, this is simply the accumulation of thousands of years of snowfall that has never melted. Even in the snowiest years, most polar regions receive only three or four inches of snow annually, an amount that is equal to about a half an inch of rain.

Shaping the Desert

The windblown snowdrifts that form at the North and South Poles can resemble the patterns in the sand of the driest deserts. And wind does play a large role in forming the desert landscape. In hot deserts, persistent winds can create towering sand dunes. These huge hills of sand can reach heights of 650 feet in the Sahara, Arabian, and Iranian Deserts. In the Sonoran

Desert of Arizona, California, and Mexico, the winds blast sand against cliffs, cutting fascinating jumbles of stair steps, ledges, and jagged rock formations.

Although rain is scarce, it too cuts and shapes the desert. Pouring rain can turn bone-dry streambeds into raging rivers within minutes. These flash floods can wash away huge boulders, medium-size rocks, and tiny pebbles, along with tons of sandy soil called silt.

The raging rivers churn down canyons and create temporary lakes, called playas, in low-lying basins. When the sun returns, the playas evaporate within weeks, leaving behind sand, clay, silt, and minerals such as salt.

Formed by evaporation and silt, playas are some of the flattest landforms on Earth. They are also very hard. The sixty-five-square-mile playa called Rogers Lake in the Mojave Desert has been used as a landing site for the space shuttle, which weighs over eighty-six tons.

The Power of Dew

Even tiny amounts of water can reshape the desert. This happens when drops of dew and fog seep into cracks in cliffs and boulders. The rock becomes slowly fragmented, pieces break off, and, eventually, giant boulders are reduced to sand.

The delicate balance between wet and dry, hot and cold, allows the earth's fragile deserts to take many forms. From the lifeless snowdrifts of Antarctica to the cactus-covered mountains of the Sonoran Desert,

The Sonoran Desert of Arizona is covered with cacti and other plants that produce colorful flowers.

there is a never-ending battle between sun, wind, rain, and snow. And within that clash of forces, nature forms some of the most extreme terrain on Earth.

Chapter 2

Plants in the Desert

Deserts may be some of the harshest environments on Earth, but they also contain a wide variety of trees, flowers, grasses, and cacti. These plants grow in places where rain is scarce, the sun is punishing, the wind raw, and temperatures often seesaw between extreme hot and cold.

In some places, lack of water combined with intense heat has created a dead zone where no plants can survive. This is the case among the wind-whipped peaks of salt and sand in the Atacama Desert in Peru. In most other deserts, however, plants can survive where even the slightest amount of precipitation is found.

Surviving the Sun

Like all plants, desert plants need sun and water to live. Too much or too little of these threatens a plant's survival. Because most deserts have lots of sun and very little water, plants have had to adapt so that the burning rays of the sun do as little damage as possible. For example, the desert broom of North Africa and the paloverde tree of North and South America produce only tiny leaves, little more than $\frac{1}{32}$ of an inch

Quiver trees grow out of the rocky soil in a southern African desert.

wide. Even in the hot sun such tiny leaves lose little water to evaporation. Other desert plants, such as the ephedra of the Kara-Kum Desert in Kazakhstan have no leaves at all. They rely instead on their green stems for **photosynthesis**, a process in which plants convert sunlight into food.

Throughout Australia the leaves of the eucalyptus tree have a white, waxy coating. This acts like a mirror that reflects the sun's rays away from the plant. Eucalyptus leaves also droop down toward the ground so that they have less surface exposed to sunshine.

Cacti, such as the barrel cactus found in the American Southwest, lessen their sun exposure by pointing their narrow trunks nearly straight up so the sun only falls on the top.

When the Rain Comes

Although plants can lessen the harmful effects of the sun, they must also soak up as much liquid as possible from rain, dew, fog, and snow.

Plants such as the Sturt's desert pea in Australia and the evening primrose of the Mojave have a simple method of survival. They live only as tiny seeds in the ground, waiting months—or sometimes years—before a soaking rainstorm brings them to life. Once it rains, millions of these seeds quickly sprout. The plants develop roots, stems, leaves, and flowers all within a few weeks. When they bloom, the wildflowers decorate the desert in the colors of the rainbow, covering the dull sand with pink, red, purple, yellow, and orange

White primrose and other desert flowers cover a Mojave Desert hillside.

flowers. Within six to eight weeks, the plants produce another crop of seeds for the next generation, then wither and die.

Succulents such as yucca, cactus, and jade plant make the most of desert rains by absorbing water with their roots. This precious liquid is then stored within the leaves and stems of the plant. The aloe, native to the African desert, can suck up an amazing amount of

The giant saguaro's knifelike needles (inset) prevent animals from biting into the cactus and stealing the water stored inside.

water in its thick, spongy leaves. Aloe leaves can swell to a height of sixty feet after a rainstorm.

The giant saguaro cactus of the Sonoran Desert is another succulent that has developed amazing survival techniques. Saguaros conserve energy and need little water because they grow very slowly. It takes the saguaro up to one hundred years to reach its full height of fifty feet.

The saguaro's water-drinking roots are only a few inches beneath the soil, but they spread out in a ring fifty feet in diameter around the cactus. When it rains, these roots channel water to the fleshy tissue inside the saguaro. This tissue is pleated like an accordion and can absorb 250 gallons of water during a single drenching rainstorm. This is enough to fill five average bathtubs. During times of drought a full-grown saguaro can store almost 1,000 gallons of water. With all that stored water, the saguaro could weigh eight thousand pounds, which is about equal to the weight of two full-size pickup trucks.

The knifelike needles that bristle on the saguaro and other cacti prevent animals from biting into them and stealing the stored water. The needles serve several other purposes as well. Some are colored white or silver, which helps them reflect the sun's rays away from the plant while also providing shade for the stem beneath. Needles often point toward the ground, which allows them to direct dew, fog, or light rain downward where it can be absorbed by the plant's thirsty roots.

Water from Rivers and Oases

Some desert plants do not need rain at all. Instead, they send their roots deep underground to water that flows in basins called **aquifers**. This is seen in Africa, where water from rainy regions drains into the aquifers beneath the Sahara Desert. In a few places, the water reaches the surface and supports a wide variety of plant and animal life in green, fertile areas called **oases**.

These areas can be small ponds or large riverlike watering holes hundreds of miles long. One Saharan oasis is five hundred miles long. Because it is surrounded by palm trees, it is known as the Street of Palms. In colder deserts like the Gobi, oases can support trees such as birch, poplar, and elm. These trees can send out roots hundreds of feet in order to tap into oasis water.

Although many deserts have oases, some also have life-giving rivers that flow through them. Some are great rivers, such as the Nile in Egypt, that flow year-

A shepherd tends his flock of sheep and goats in a Gobi Desert river valley.

round. Other rivers are fed by rain and melting snow in faraway mountains and may dry up or stand in isolated pools for part of the year. Wherever there are rivers, however, plants will grow. Where the Colorado River flows through the Grand Canyon on the southeastern edge of the Great Basin, bright green Fremont cottonwood trees can be seen shimmering on sandy beaches along with pink-flowered tamarisks, and graceful willows. These thirsty trees sink roots into the river and have a steady source of liquid nourishment.

Unlike the cottonwood and tamarisk, mesquite bushes may live far from the riverbanks. These bushes survive in the driest areas because of their long water-seeking roots. One mesquite bush in the Grand Canyon was found to have a root system that tunneled down 175 feet to find water deep underground.

Only the Strong Survive

In the desert, all plants must obtain water to grow. Plants that thrive in this harsh environment have developed a variety of ways to soak up this precious resource. And although these desert plants bring great beauty to the barren lands, it is only the strongest of **species** that can survive under the punishing desert sun.

How Animals Survive in the Desert

Animals that live in the desert have had to adapt to an environment with extreme temperatures, little shade, and almost no water. And like all living creatures, they need food and water to survive. To obtain these important resources—and avoid too much sun—desert dwellers have developed many interesting patterns of behavior.

The biggest challenge for a desert creature is to keep its body temperature from becoming too hot. This is difficult for animals that must crawl or walk across the desert surface, where it can be much hotter than the air temperature. Surface temperatures can rise to two hundred degrees Fahrenheit in places like Death Valley. These temperatures can kill reptiles such as lizards and snakes because they are cold-blooded. (This means that their bodies are the same temperature as their surroundings.) When a reptile's temperature rises above 104 degrees, it can die. For this reason, most desert reptiles live in holes in the ground called burrows. Because of their location underground, out of the sun, these burrows can be fifty to one hundred degrees cooler than the surface temperature.

Staying Cool

Small desert mammals such as rabbits, rats, mice, and other fur-bearing creatures are warm-blooded. Like

A Pacific rattlesnake coils into striking position. Snakes and other reptiles are common desert animals.

humans, they maintain a constant body temperature. Mammals, however, can become dangerously dehydrated when their bodies lose moisture in the hot sun. For this reason, many desert mammals also live in burrows. Gerbils of the African and Asian deserts, for example, dig a complex system of tunnels three to six feet below the ground. There they spend most of their days in temperatures hovering around sixty-five degrees.

Breathing and Spit

Burrowing animals sleep during the day and only hunt for food at night when temperatures drop. During the hottest months of the year, when nighttime temperatures remain high, these small mammals can stay underground for weeks at a time. They do so by slowing down their bodily functions to conserve energy. This process, in which an animal's body temperature drops and its breathing and heartbeat slow, is called **estivation**. When the tiny pocket mouse enters the estivation stage, its body can cool from 102 degrees to about 62 degrees. If the outside temperature drops below freezing, the mouse's body temperature can drop as low as 43 degrees, and its breathing almost stops. When the weather warms, the mouse awakens and resumes its daily life, hunting for seeds to eat.

Some animals that sleep in burrows stay cool by wetting down their bodies. In Australia, the desert wallaby produces large amounts of saliva when it gets too hot. To cool down, the wallaby uses its tongue to spread its spit all over its body. Koalas do the same thing, licking their paws and rubbing saliva on their faces when their body temperature rises above ninety-nine degrees.

Dealing with the Heat

Larger mammals such as the African ibex, a species of goat, and the addax, a type of antelope, cannot burrow in the ground. Instead, these creatures spend their days in caves or in the shade of rocky cliffs.

Both the desert wallaby (below) and the koala (right) cover themselves with spit to stay cool.

Adapting For Survival

Desert
Bighorn
Sheep

Gila
Woodpecker

Western
Diamondback
Rattlesnake

Desert (Kit)
Foxes

Desert Horned
Lizard

Venomous
Scorpion

Round Tail
Ground Squirrel

Some birds also take advantage of shady cliffs and caves. Others sit almost motionless through the heat of the day in shrubs or bushes. Birds such as the Gila woodpecker of the Sonoran Desert peck holes in saguaros. They can then escape the heat by climbing inside the cool, moist cacti. The six-inch-tall elf owl—the smallest owl in the world—often moves into the cacti holes that have been abandoned by the woodpeckers.

High-flying birds have an easier time escaping the blistering desert environment. Eagles in the Kalahari, for example, can soar more than fifteen hundred feet in the air. At this elevation, temperatures can be as much as one hundred degrees cooler than the baking desert floor.

Some creatures only need to raise their bodies a small distance from the searing desert surface. For example, ants in the Sahara walk with their legs as straight as possible to lift their bodies just a few centimeters higher, where it is slightly cooler.

How the Camel Survives

The long legs of the camel keep its body about five feet off the ground, where it can be seventy degrees cooler. And the camel has developed several other features that allow it to thrive in the desert. For example, the feet of the camel are broad, flat, and leathery pads with two toes on each foot. When the camel walks, the pads keep the animal from sinking into the soft sand. To protect its eyes, a camel has two pairs of eyelashes—one very long, curly pair to shade its eyes from the sun and one shorter, straight pair to protect its eyes from the sand. It is the camel's hump, however, that allows it to survive for days without water.

The single hump of a common camel is filled with twenty to thirty pounds of fat, which also contains water. (A two-humped, or Bactrian, camel carries up to fifty pounds of fat.) This fat acts as a store of food that allows the camel to go ten days without eating. During this long period between meals, every pound of fat digested for energy also provides one pound of water. This allows the camel to go seven days without drinking. When the animal does finally arrive at an oasis, it can swallow over twenty-seven gallons of water in a few minutes—enough to fill about half of an average bathtub.

Cooling Water

Thousands of other animals depend on desert water holes as well. In the American Southwest, water holes attract skunks, rodents, squirrels, mule deer, badgers, weasels, and wild pigs called javelinas. During dry months, these oases can become extremely crowded with animal visitors desperate for water. At these times even natural enemies, such as foxes and coyotes, tolerate one another in order to drink.

Some desert animals get all the liquid they need from their food. Toads, for example, feed at night, using their long, sticky tongues to slurp up ants and other insects. Since insect bodies are about 75 percent water, toads never need to visit water holes. Toads also have porous skin that allows them to absorb fog and dew from the surrounding air.

Few desert creatures can utilize fog the way darkling beetles do in the Namib Desert. Although rain rarely falls on this parched wilderness, fog does blow

The two-humped Bactrian camel can go several days without drinking or eating.

in from the neighboring Atlantic Ocean. The beetles take advantage of this situation by perching motionless atop sand dunes with their hind legs in the air and their backs toward the sea. This action, known as "fog basking," allows the few droplets of moisture from the fog to condense on the beetles' backs and run down through ridges in their bodies into their open mouths.

A fog-basking beetle slurps up water that has collected on its back.

The desert bighorn sheep is one of the thousands of animal species that live in the desert.

Rich in Wildlife

Fog-basking beetles are but one of the five thousand species of insects, birds, reptiles, amphibians, and **mammals** that call the desert home. Some cover themselves in spit, live off the fat in their humps, or sleep the summer away in underground tunnels. Their methods of coping are as rich and varied as the terrain itself. And despite conditions that would kill most animals, creatures of the desert thrive, eating and drinking just enough to survive.

Chapter 4

People of the Desert

The desert is a harsh environment for people as well as plants and animals. The lack of water combined with searing temperatures pose a great challenge to people who live in the desert. Under normal conditions, a human cannot survive more than three days without water. In the hot desert sun, where it may be 120 degrees Fahrenheit, the average adult can die from the heat in a single day. In such high temperatures a person loses up to a quart of water an hour by sweating. Within a few hours, this creates extreme thirst. Meanwhile, the body can lose up to eighteen pounds of fluid through perspiration. By nightfall death may occur if no drinking water is available to replace the lost fluids.

Despite these hardships, people have lived in the world's deserts for thousands of years. Today, over 240 million people—4 percent of the world's population— live in desert environments.

A Mongolian woman holds a wooden rake in the Gobi Desert. Today, over 240 million people live in deserts.

Irrigating Crops

The first cities in the desert were built in present-day Iraq about six thousand years ago. The desert dwellers were able to make the deserts bloom by digging ditches that carried water to their fields from the Tigris and Euphrates Rivers. This method of farming, called **irrigation**, improved over the centuries. By 1750 B.C., Iraq had a system of brick-lined canals. These canals irrigated fields that spread over ten thousand square miles of desert, which is an area about the size of Vermont.

Dams built from mud and rock helped desert dwellers store water for the driest times of year. The

Irrigation is still used in Egypt today.

dams created lakes. Water from the lakes could be diverted to fields through irrigation canals. With such a system in place, 20 million people were able to thrive in a desert where less than ten inches of rain fell every year. In this manner, ancient people were able to grow a wide variety of food crops, including wheat, lentils, fruits, nuts, and vegetables.

People today still depend on dams and irrigation for growing crops in desert regions. For example, 96 percent of Egypt is desert. Nearly all of Egypt's 65 million people live along the Nile River. They depend on crops grown with irrigation water from the river.

Complex systems of pumps, pipes, and channels transport water from rivers and lakes to people in many large desert cities. These include Cairo, Egypt; Phoenix, Arizona; and San Diego, California.

Water from Wells

Rivers and lakes are not the only sources of water that have allowed people to live in deserts. The Cahuilla tribes of south-central California once relied on water wells for survival. They dug wells to collect droplets of water that oozed out of the desert floor. Wherever there was a tiny spring or even a seep of a few drops bubbling up from under the ground, the Cahuilla built long, narrow trenches down to it.

The Cahuilla were able to avoid the sun by living in houses made from the reedlike tule plant. They also used palm fronds, mesquite branches, and other local desert plants. In Cahuilla villages, family members might construct two or three such shelters and connect them with roofed walkways. This allowed people to perform chores out of the sun and wind. In the hot summer a plaster made from mud could be applied to the huts to keep them cool. In the hottest days, the Cahuilla moved into cool caves. In this manner, they were able to survive thousands of years in the desert heat.

Life in the Kalahari

Some desert cultures, such as the Bushmen in the Kalahari, still depend on well water. The Bushmen have lived in the Kalahari for more than thirty thousand years. Today there are about fifty thousand Bushmen, but only around two thousand continue to live in their traditional manner in the African countries of Botswana and Namibia.

In Namibia many Bushmen live in an area called Nyae Nyae, where underground aquifers feed about thirty permanent wells, called boreholes. These wells provide water for the tribes and also attract a wide variety of game animals such as rabbits, porcupines, antelopes, and ostriches. One ostrich can weigh over three hundred pounds and provide enough food for days. Extra meat is dried in the sun for later use, and empty ostrich eggs, as big as balloons, are used to store water.

Detailed knowledge of desert plants has also helped the Bushmen find both food and water in the desert. The Bushmen use over one hundred species of

Kalahari Bushmen (above) use ostrich eggs to collect water from a desert waterhole (inset).

plants for food. Women use sticks to dig up edible roots and potato-like tubers. Water can also be obtained from the tsama melon and the gemsbok cucumber.

Sahara Survival

Rivers, well water, and plants are important to the survival of most desert peoples. In the Sahara Desert of North Africa, animals are also a central part of life.

More than 6 million Bedouins live in the deserts of northern Africa and the Middle East. They occupy parts of the Sahara, Syrian, and Arabian Deserts. In ancient times, these people were **nomads**. They had no fixed home and moved from place to place in search

A Bedouin man offers an evening prayer. More than 6 million Bedouins live in the Middle East and Africa.

of food, water, and grazing land. Today, only about 180,000, or 3 percent, of the Bedouins, still wander the desert in nomadic tribes as their ancestors once did.

Traditionally, the Bedouins have tended small herds of camels, sheep, goats, and horses. These animals are central to Bedouin survival in the searing deserts. The tribes eat the meat of the animals and obtain milk from the goats.

Traveling in the Desert

Camels play a central role in Bedouin life. When tribes want to move, they assemble long trains, or caravans, of camels, tying the animals nose-to-tail with long ropes. Each animal can carry a rider on its back or up to 650 pounds of supplies. As camel caravans cross the desert, young men use horses and donkeys to herd along the flocks of sheep and goats.

Most often, Bedouin travel is based on the seasons. Winter rains create a carpet of green grasses in some parts of the desert. This provides grazing land for live-stock. In the heat of the summer, the Bedouins travel from oasis to oasis. When grasses are eaten at one oasis, the camels are assembled and the tribe moves on.

The Bedouins find protection from the extreme heat by wrapping themselves in layers of cloth. These flowing robes absorb the sun's hot rays and allow cooling breezes to circulate beneath. Men wind cloths called *kufiyyas* around their heads and necks to prevent moisture loss that can lead to heatstroke. These garments also shield the face against the harsh, dry sand.

Women wear loose black or blue dresses that cover the body and shield them from blowing sand. Bedouin headdresses cover the head, throat, and forehead and offer protection from the sun. Veils keep out dust and sand during sandstorms.

Bedouins live in tents made from cloth woven from camel hair. The sides of these low, square tents may be

A Bedouin woman, dressed in a traditional blue dress and black headdress, prepares a pot of tea.

Deserts have been home to people, plants, and animals for thousands of years.

rolled up to let in cooling breezes or pulled down tight during cold weather and sandstorms.

A Fragile Ecosystem

People, plants, and animals have long survived the harsh desert environment. Although many dangers exist in the hot, arid landscapes, they are filled with incredible beauty. And they are also places where people have been able to build amazing cultures in an extremely demanding environment for thousand of years.

Glossary

aquifer: An underground bed of earth, gravel, or stone that stores water.

continent: One of the main landmasses of the earth, including Africa, Antarctica, Asia, Australia, Europe, North America, and South America.

environment: The combination of conditions that affect and influence the growth, development, and survival of plants and animals.

equator: The imaginary circle around the center of the earth, halfway between the North and South Poles.

estivation: A condition of rest in some animals during the summer or months of drought, marked by a slowing of the bodily functions.

evaporate: To convert or change into a vapor. When ocean water evaporates, it forms rain clouds.

habitat: The area or type of environment in which an organism normally lives.

irrigate: To supply dry land with water by diverting it through ditches, pipes, or sprinklers.

mammal: Warm-blooded creatures that have a covering of hair and whose young are born alive and are nourished by mothers with milk.

nomads: People with no fixed homes who move according to the seasons in search of food, water, and grazing land.

nutrient: A mineral or chemical that provides a source of nourishment, especially in food.

oases: Fertile or green areas of a desert, made so by the availability of water.

photosynthesis: The process by which green plants convert energy from sunlight into food and oxygen.

precipitation: Any form of water, such as rain, snow, sleet, or hail, that falls to the earth's surface.

species: A category or type of plant or animal.

succulents: Plants that have thick, fleshy, water-storing leaves or stems.

For Further Exploration

Books

Jim Arnosky, *Watching Desert Wildlife*. Washington, DC: National Geographic Society, 1998. A colorful book about desert lizards, birds, deer, owls, and other creatures.

Allan Fowler, *Living in a Desert*. New York: Childrens, 2000. This book discusses people who live in desert areas of the world and how the environment affects their lives.

Jen Green, *Desert Animals*. Bath, UK: Dempsey Parr, 2000. The stories of animals, birds, and insects that live in desert environments are presented in this book.

Miranda MacQuitty, *Desert*. New York: Dorling Kindersley, 2000. This book offers large pictures and exciting facts about dwellers of the desert.

Websites

Deserts USA 2003 (www.desertusa.com/index.html). A website with information about the geography, plants, animals, and hiking trails of the Mojave, Sonoran, Great Basin, and other North American deserts.

MBGnet, "Desert" (http://mbgnet.mobot.org/sets/ desert). A colorful site with pictures and information linking types of deserts, desert locations, plants and animals, and more.

Sonoran Desert Educational Center, "Sonoran Desert Kids" (www.co.pima.az.us/cmo/sdcp/kids). A site with information about the Arizona desert. Links connect desert stories, artwork, quizzes, and coloring pages and an endangered species card game that can be printed out.

Index

paloverde trees, 15–16
Patagonian Desert (Argentina), 8
people
  ancient, 34–35
  number of, living in deserts, 33
  temperatures and survival of, 5, 32
Peru Current, 7
plants
  along rivers, 21
  leaves of, 15–16
  in oases, 20
  rain and, 16–17
  used by Bushmen, 37
  see also specific types
playas, 12
pocket mice, 24
polar deserts, 11
poplar trees, 20
precipitation
  amount of, defines desert, 4
  in cold deserts, 6
  flash floods and, 12
  plants and, 16–17
  in polar deserts, 11

rainfall, 4, 16–17
rain-shadow effect, 8–9, 11
Reno, Nevada, 11
reptiles, 23
rivers, 20–21
Rogers Lake, 12

saguaro cacti, 18–19

Sahara Desert (Libya)
  ants in, 27
  aquifers beneath, 19–20
  Bedouins of, 38–41
  ocean currents and, 7–8
  sand hills in, 11
  temperatures in, 5
seeds, 16–17
Sierra Nevada (California), 8–9
snow, 6, 11
Sonoran Desert (United States)
  birds of, 27
  landscape of, 11–12
space shuttle, 12
Street of Palms, 20
Sturt's desert peas, 16–17
succulents, 17–18
  see also cacti
surface temperatures, 22–23
Syrian Desert, 38–41

tamarisk trees, 21
temperatures
  of cold deserts, 6
  on desert surface, 22–23, 27
  human survival and, 5, 32
  of polar deserts, 11
Tigris River, 34–35
toads, 28–29

wallabies, 24–25
wells, 35–36
winds, 8, 11–12

yucca, 17